Fox

by Iain Gray

79 Main Street, Newtongrange,
Midlothian EH22 4NA
Tel: 0131 344 0414   Fax: 0845 075 6085
E-mail: info@lang-syne.co.uk
www.langsyneshop.co.uk

Design by Dorothy Meikle
Printed by Blissetts
© Lang Syne Publishers Ltd 2021

All rights reserved. No part of this publication may be reproduced, stored or introduced into a retrieval system, or transmitted in any form or by any means (electronic, mechanical, photocopying, recording or otherwise) without the prior written permission of Lang Syne Publishers Ltd.

ISBN 978-1-85217-782-9

Fox

MOTTO:
Be faithful

CREST:
A fox

NAME variations include:
    Foxe
    Foxx

Chapter one:

The origins of popular surnames

by George Forbes and Iain Gray

***If you don't know where you came from, you won't know where you're going** is a frequently quoted observation and one that has a particular resonance today when there has been a marked upsurge in interest in genealogy, with increasing numbers of people curious to trace their family roots.*

Main sources for genealogical research include census returns and official records of births, marriages and deaths – and the key to unlocking the detail they contain is obviously a family surname, one that has been 'inherited' and passed from generation to generation.

No matter our station in life, we all have a surname – but it was not until about the middle of the fourteenth century that the practice of being identified by a particular surname became commonly established throughout the British Isles.

Previous to this, it was normal for a person to be identified through the use of only a forename.

But as population gradually increased and there were many more people with the same forename, surnames were adopted to distinguish one person, or community, from another.

Many common English surnames are patronymic in origin, meaning they stem from the forename of one's father – with 'Johnson,' for example, indicating 'son of John.'

It was the Normans, in the wake of their eleventh century conquest of Anglo-Saxon England, a pivotal moment in the nation's history, who first brought surnames into usage – although it was a gradual process.

For the Normans, these were names initially based on the title of their estates, local villages and chateaux in France to distinguish and identify these landholdings.

Such grand descriptions also helped enhance the prestige of these warlords and generally glorify their lofty positions high above the humble serfs slaving away below in the pecking order who had only single names, often with Biblical connotations as in Pierre and Jacques.

The only descriptive distinctions among the peasantry concerned their occupations, like 'Pierre the swineherd' or 'Jacques the ferryman.'

Roots of surnames that came into usage in England not only included Norman-French, but also Old French, Old Norse, Old English, Middle English, German, Latin, Greek, Hebrew and the Gaelic languages of the Celts.

The Normans themselves were originally Vikings, or 'Northmen', who raided, colonised and eventually settled down around the French coastline.

They had sailed up the Seine in their long-boats in 900AD under their ferocious leader Rollo and ruled the roost in north eastern France before sailing over to conquer England in 1066 under Duke William of Normandy – better known to posterity as William the Conqueror, or King William I of England.

Granted lands in the newly-conquered England, some of their descendants later acquired territories in Wales, Scotland and Ireland – taking not only their own surnames, but also the practice of adopting a surname, with them.

But it was in England where Norman rule and custom first impacted, particularly in relation to the adoption of surnames.

This is reflected in the famous *Domesday Book*, a massive survey of much of England and Wales, ordered by William I, to determine who owned what, what it was worth and therefore how much they were liable to pay in taxes to the voracious Royal Exchequer.

Completed in 1086 and now held in the National Archives in Kew, London, 'Domesday' was an Old English word meaning 'Day of Judgement.'

This was because, in the words of one contemporary chronicler, "its decisions, like those of the Last Judgement, are unalterable."

It had been a requirement of all those English landholders – from the richest to the poorest – that they identify themselves for the purposes of the survey and for future reference by means of a surname.

This is why the *Domesday Book*, although written in Latin as was the practice for several centuries with both civic and ecclesiastical records, is an invaluable source for the early appearance of a wide range of English surnames.

Several of these names were coined in connection with occupations.

These include Baker and Smith, while Cooks, Chamberlains, Constables and Porters were to be found carrying out duties in large medieval households.

The church's influence can be found in names such as Bishop, Friar and Monk while the popular name of Bennett derives from the late fifth to mid-sixth century Saint Benedict, founder of the Benedictine order of monks.

The early medical profession is represented by Barber, while businessmen produced names that include Merchant and Sellers.

Down at the village watermill, the names that cropped up included Millar/Miller, Walker and Fuller, while other self-explanatory trades included Cooper, Tailor, Mason and Wright.

Even the scenery was utilised as in Moor, Hill, Wood and Forrest – while the hunt and the chase supplied names that include Hunter, Falconer, Fowler and Fox.

Colours are also a source of popular surnames, as in Black, Brown, Gray/Grey, Green and White, and would have denoted the colour of the clothing the person habitually wore or, apart from the obvious exception of 'Green', one's hair colouring or even complexion.

The surname Red developed into Reid, while

Blue was rare and no-one wanted to be associated with yellow.

Rather self-important individuals took surnames that include Goodman and Wiseman, while physical attributes crept into surnames such as Small and Little.

Many families proudly boast the heraldic device known as a Coat of Arms, as featured on our front cover.

The central motif of the Coat of Arms would originally have been what was borne on the shield of a warrior to distinguish himself from others on the battlefield.

Not featured on the Coat of Arms, but highlighted on page three, is the family motto and related crest – with the latter frequently different from the central motif.

Adding further variety to the rich cultural heritage that is represented by surnames is the appearance in recent times in lists of the 100 most common names found in England of ones that include Khan, Patel and Singh – names that have proud roots in the vast sub-continent of India.

Echoes of a far distant past can still be found in our surnames and they can be borne with pride in commemoration of our forebears.

Chapter two:

Honours and distinction

A surname of straightforward origin – deriving as it does from the animal of the name – 'Fox' has been present from earliest times and may have developed as an occupational name for someone involved in the hunt, or the chase.

Ranked 67th in some lists of the 100 most common surnames found in the United Kingdom today, it enters the historical record from an early date, with Sir Stephen Fox a prominent Royalist during the seventeenth century English Civil War.

King Charles I had incurred the wrath of Parliament by his insistence on the 'divine right' of monarchs, and added to this was the fear of Catholic 'subversion' against the state and the king's stubborn refusal to grant demands for religious and constitutional concessions.

Matters came to a head with the outbreak of the Civil War in 1642, with Parliamentary forces, known as the New Model Army and commanded by Oliver Cromwell and Sir Thomas Fairfax, arrayed against the Royalist army of the king.

In what became an increasingly bloody and complex conflict, spreading to Scotland and Ireland and with rapidly shifting loyalties on both sides, the 49-year-old king was eventually captured and executed in January of 1649 on the orders of Parliament.

Stephen Fox, meanwhile, born in 1627 in Farley, Wiltshire, went from humble roots as a farmer's son to accrue great honours under the tragic king's son, Charles II, when he was restored to the throne in 1660.

Entering the household of Algernon Percy, 10th Earl of Northumberland, he was later present at the battle of Worcester in September of 1651 when a Scots army that had rallied to the cause of Charles was defeated by Cromwell and the king forced to flee into continental exile.

Accompanying him on his flight, Fox gained the monarch's trust to the extent that he was appointed manager of the royal household-in-exile, with responsibilities that included the onerous task of managing its precarious finances.

One contemporary source described him as being "… very well qualified with languages and all other parts of clerkship, honesty and discretion."

Also employed on a number of dangerous diplomatic missions, Fox was rewarded by a grateful Charles on his restoration with honours that included a knighthood and the highly lucrative post of Paymaster of the Forces.

Serving for a time as MP (Member of Parliament) for Salisbury, he died in 1716.

Born in 1624, the son of a Leicestershire weaver, George Fox was a founder in the 1650s of the Religious Society of Friends, the Christian denomination better known as the Quakers.

Distinguished by their plain dress, teetotalism, refusal to swear oaths, participate in wars and opposition to slavery, Fox and other early adherents of the faith were frequently imprisoned for refusing to swear the Oath of Allegiance to the Crown.

They acquired the nickname 'Quakers' when Fox famously told a judge 'to tremble at the name of the Lord'.

Fox died in 1691 and Quakerism established firm roots, including in what became the American state of Pennsylvania – named after the leading English Quaker and settler William Penn.

One particularly noted family of the Fox name had its roots in Falmouth, Cornwall, and came to boast an array of talent that included businessmen, scientists, inventors and writers.

Of the Quaker faith – as were his descendants – Robert Were Fox, born in 1768 and known as R.W. Fox the Elder, was the wealthy businessman who, through his marriage to Elizabeth Tregelles, came to found before his death in 1848 the famous Fox dynasty.

His eldest son, known as Robert Were Fox the Younger, was the geologist, physicist and inventor born in Falmouth in 1789.

In addition to working as a partner in the family's shipping firm and acting as general manager for a time of its Perran Iron Foundry, at Perranarworthal, as a scientist he invented a special compass to measure magnetic dip at sea – thereby aiding polar navigation – and also worked on determining the temperature of the earth.

A Fellow of the scientific think-tank the Royal Society, a member of the British Association for the Advancement of Science and instrumental in the development of the Royal Cornwall Polytechnic Society, he died in 1877.

His younger brother Charles Fox, born in 1797 and who died in 1878, was the scientist who, in addition to working in the family's shipping brokerage, iron foundry, and copper mining and smelting interests, in 1841 co-founded the Lander Prizes for essays on, and maps of, geographical areas.

The founder in 1859 of the Miners' Association of Cornwall and Devon, he also served for a time as president of the Royal Geological Society of Cornwall in addition to being responsible along with other family members for the development of a number of gardens.

These include Trebah Gardens, Glendurgan, and the gardens of Rosehill and Penjerrick, in Falmouth.

Meanwhile, through his marriage to Maria Barclay, his older brother Robert Were the Younger was the father of Caroline, Barclay and Anna Maria Fox.

It was along with her brother Barclay, born in 1817 and who died in 1855, that Caroline, born in 1819 and who died in 1871, compiled a remarkable series of journals chronicling their lives and times.

First published in 1881, they were republished more than ninety years later, in 1972.

Caroline and Barclay's older sister Anna

Maria, born in 1816, is recognised today as having been instrumental before her death in 1897 of her native Falmouth's artistic and cultural development.

One particularly colourful member of the extended family of the Foxes of Falmouth and one whose lifestyle no doubt raised a few eyebrows among his rather more staid Quaker relatives was Charles Masson Fox.

Born in Falmouth in 1866, he became established as a respectable businessman, serving on the board of the family's firm of shipping agents and as a partner in its timber concern Fox Stanton and Company.

Described by a contemporary as "a friendly man, mellow, lovable, bringing peace and comfort and serene joy with him", Fox was nevertheless in many ways a troubled man.

In an age when homosexuality was a penal offence, he was 'discreetly but actively' gay – and this was to lead to the destruction of his business and social reputation in Falmouth.

In 1909 he visited more liberally-minded Venice in the company of a friend, James Cockerton, and they met the English writer Frederick Rolfe – also known as 'Baron Corvo' who, in his *Venice Letters* not only vividly described the city's gay subculture but also 'outed' the hapless Fox by naming him.

To add to his woes, in 1912 he was blackmailed by a woman who falsely accused him of seducing her 16-year-old son.

In a subsequent court case, the woman was found guilty of blackmail and sentenced to five years' imprisonment and her son to one year – but, although Fox was blameless, he was shunned by business colleagues and the Falmouth social set.

Settling for a time in London, he not only enjoyed a new social life but also became prominent in the highly cerebral world of chess.

A leading figure in the development of the British Chess Problem Society, he is regarded to this day as one of the greatest ever exponents of what is known as 'fairy chess' – involving problems with rules' variations.

He died in 1935, by which time he had become prominent worldwide in this complex field.

Chapter three:

Politics and invention

Bearers of the Fox name have been prominent, and remain prominent, in the often cut-throat world of politics.

Despite having led a rather dissolute early life, Henry Fox became a significant figure in eighteenth century British politics.

Born in Wiltshire in 1705, his father was the seventeenth century English Royalist Sir Stephen Fox, referred to in the previous chapter.

Inheriting a substantial share of his father's wealth, Fox proceeded to rapidly squander it through his taste for high-living that included gambling.

Racking up massive debts, in a bid to escape his clamouring debtors he fled into continental exile – but fortune favoured him when he forged an intimate relationship with an older lady, discreetly described as 'a woman of fortune.'

Apparently in return for the favours that the dashing Fox bestowed on her, he was able to return to England a wealthy man.

Much to the chagrin of her family at the time,

he eloped with and, in 1744, married the young Lady Caroline Lennox, a daughter of the Duke of Richmond.

Entering politics as a Whig – as opposed to Tory – he displayed great political acumen and went on to hold high government posts that included Secretary for War.

Raised to the Peerage as Henry Fox, 1st Baron Holland of Foxley, in the County of Wiltshire, in 1763, he died eleven years later.

He was the father of Charles James Fox who, in common with his father, in his youth followed a rather reckless and dissolute lifestyle.

Following in the paternal footsteps, he incurred a vast amount of debt – at one stage the staggering amount of £120,000, equivalent to approximately £11m in today's terms.

Born in 1749, he was marked out for posterity from birth with a particularly dark and hairy complexion – leading to his father describing him as 'looking like a monkey.'

But, despite this description, he cut a dashing figure in London society, soon becoming a leading character of the fashionable group of young men known as the 'Macaroni Set' – eighteenth century 'dedicated followers of fashion' who set their own rules as to lifestyle.

Entering politics as a Whig politician and a close friend of King George III, he became highly influential despite controversial views that included support for the French Revolution.

Nicknamed "The Eyebrow" by his contemporaries because of his distinctively luxurious growth of eyebrows and an iconic figure of his times, his fame has endured. He died in 1806, while he was portrayed by the actor Jim Carter in the 1994 film *The Madness of King George* and by Michael Gambon in the 2006 *Amazing Grace* and, in 2008, in *The Duchess*.

In contemporary politics, Dr Liam Fox is the Conservative Party politician born in 1961 in the Scottish town of East Kilbride.

Having studied medicine at Glasgow University, he became a GP and then worked as a civilian army medical doctor before entering politics in 2010 as MP for North Somerset.

Posts he has held include Secretary of State for Defence from 2010 to 2011 and Secretary of State for International Trade from 2016 to 2019, while he is also author of the 2013 *Rising Tides: Facing the Challenges of a New Era*.

Born in 1927, Sir John Marcus Fox was the Conservative Party politician who served for a time as chairman of the party's influential 1922 Committee; MP for the Shipley constituency from 1970 to 1997, he died in 2002.

Bearers of the Fox name have also been prominent in the worlds of engineering and commerce.

Born in Derby in 1810, Sir Charles Fox was the English construction engineer and inventor who along with others, including Joseph Paxton, designed and built the Crystal Palace for the 1851 Great Exhibition in London.

Also involved in what was then the rapidly burgeoning railway industry, in 1832 he invented the forerunner of what is known today as the 'railway points' system.

He also constructed railway systems in South Africa, Canada and Australia.

In recognition of his outstanding contribution to the industry he was elevated to the peerage as Sir Charles Fox. He died in 1874.

Not only an engineer and industrialist but also a noted English philanthropist, Samson Fox was born in 1838 in Bradford, Yorkshire.

Very much a self-made man, this son of a

mill worker was apprenticed in a tool-making and foundry company when he was aged fifteen – and by the time he was in his late 'twenties he had established his own company, the Silver Cross Works.

Displaying a flair for invention, in 1877, after having set up the Leeds Forge Company, he developed what became renowned worldwide as 'Fox Corrugated.'

This was an ingenious device that was adapted for railway and naval engines that involved corrugating the flue pipes inside boilers to allow them to work safely at high pressures.

In 1888, Fox travelled to the United States and teamed up with the American entrepreneur 'Diamond Jim' Brady, and the pair established an enterprise to manufacture pressed iron railway carriages.

As a philanthropist, the immensely wealthy Fox set up a number of foundations that include the Royal Hall in Harrogate, in his native Yorkshire, and the Royal College of Music, in London.

The recipient of a number of honours and awards that include the gold medal of the Royal Society of Arts and the French Legion of Honour, he died in 1903.

Chapter four:

On the world stage

A member of a famous British acting dynasty, Robin Fox was the theatrical agent and actor born in London in 1913.

A grandson of the nineteenth century engineer, industrialist and philanthropist Samson Fox, referred to in the previous chapter, he was related through his mother Hilda Louise Fox, née Alcock, and his aunt Lily Hanbury to the acting dynasty of the Neilson/Hanbury family.

His mother's cousin, the actress Julia Neilson, was married to the actor Fred Terry, a brother of the famed late nineteenth century actress Ellen Terry.

Married to the actress Angela Worthington, a daughter of the playwright Frederick Lonsdale, he was the father of the leading contemporary actors James Fox and Edward Fox, the theatrical agent and producer Robert Fox, and the grandfather of the actors Laurence, Lydia, Emilia, Freddie and Jack Fox.

Robin Fox died in 1971, by which time his son William James Fox, born in London in 1939 and better known as **James Fox**, had become an established actor of the big screen.

His first screen credit was the 1950 *The Miniver Story*, followed by the 1964 *The Loneliness of the Long Distance Runner*, while also in that year he won a BAFTA Award for Most Promising Newcomer for his role in *The Servant*.

Further screen credits throughout the 1960s and 1970s include the 1965 *Those Magnificent Men in their Flying Machines* and, from the same year, *King Rat*, the 1968 *Isadora* and the 1970 *Performance*.

Taking a break of almost ten years from acting following a nervous breakdown, he returned to the screen for roles in films that include the 1984 *A Passage to India*, while other credits include the 1992 BBC play *A Question of Attribution*, the 1993 film *The Remains of the Day* and the 2004 *Agatha Christie – Death on the Nile*.

Also having appeared in the 2010 thriller *Cleanskin* and the role of King George V in the 2011 *W.E.*, and following a relationship with the actress Sarah Miles, he has been married since 1973 to Mary Elizabeth Piper.

Three of their five children are the actors Laurence, Lydia and Jack Fox.

Born in Yorkshire in 1978, **Laurence Fox** worked for a time as a gardener and then in an office before studying at the Royal Academy of Dramatic Art (RADA).

After having appeared in a number of theatrical productions he has secured screen credits in films that include the 2001 *The Hole* and, from the same year, *Gosford Park*.

Married since 2006 to the actress and singer Billie Piper, on television he is best known for his role of Detective Sergeant James Hathaway in the *Morse* detective drama spin-off *Lewis*.

Also a musician, he became the subject of controversy in 2020 over remarks he made that were deemed critical of aspects of 'political correctness'.

His sister **Lydia Fox**, born in 1979 and also, following her marriage to the actor, director and writer Richard Ayoade known as Lydia Ayoade, is the actress and producer with credits that include the 2006 *Someone Else* and the television medical drama *Holby City*.

Her brother **Jack Fox**, born in London in 1985, is the actor whose television credits include the role of Ralph in *Fresh Meat*.

His paternal uncle is **Edward Fox**, born in

1937, and whose many screen credits include the 1969 *Oh! What a Lovely War*, the 1969 *Battle of Britain* and, from 1973, *The Day of the Jackal*.

Winner of a BAFTA Award for Best Supporting Actor for his role in the 1971 *The Go-Between*, other credits include the 1977 *A Bridge Too Far* – for which he won another BAFTA Award for Best Supporting Actor – the 1978 *Force Ten from Navarone*, the 1982 *Ghandi* and the 2004 *Stage Beauty*, while he also portrayed King Edward VIII in the 1978 television drama *Edward & Mrs Simpson*.

The recipient of an OBE for his services to theatre and British cinema, he is the father through his first marriage to the actress Tracy Reed of the actors Emilia and Freddie Fox.

Born in London in 1974, **Emilia Fox** has big screen credits that include the 2005 *Keeping Mum* and the 2008 *Flashbacks of a Fool*, while those in television include the role of Dr Nikki Alexander in the crime drama *Silent Witness*.

Her brother **Freddie Fox**, born in 1989, has film credits that include the 2011 *The Three Musketeers* and the 2015 *Frankenstein* and ones in television that include *Worried About the Boy*, *The Mystery of Edwin Drood*, *Cucumber* and *Banana*.

His paternal uncle is the theatre and film producer **Robert Fox**, born in 1953, whose theatrical productions include *The Breath of Life* and *Hedda Gabler*, while film credits include the 2002 *The Hours* and, from 2004, *Closer*.

On North American shores, **Michael J. Fox** is the Canadian-American actor best known for his role from 1985 to 1990 of Marty McFly in the *Back to the Future* trilogy of films.

Born in 1961 in Edmonton, Alberta, other screen credits include the 1991 *Doc Hollywood* and the 1994 *Greedy*, while he won two Screen Actors Guild Awards, two Golden Globes and three Emmys for his role from 1996 to 2001 in the television series *Spin City*.

Diagnosed with Parkinson's disease in 1991 and creator of the Michael J. Fox Foundation in 2010 for research towards finding a cure for the disease, he was appointed an Officer of the Order of Canada (OC) in 2010, and is honoured on both the Canada Walk of Fame and the Hollywood Walk of Fame.

Back on British shores, **Bernard Fox** is the stage name of the retired Welsh television and film actor born Bernard Lawson in Port Talbot, Wales, in 1927.

His credits include the 1958 film *A Night to Remember*, concerning the sinking of the cruise liner *Titanic*, and its 1997 remake *Titanic*, while television credits include *Hogan's Heroes*, *Bewitched* and *Columbo*.

Born in 1979 in Truro, Cornwall, **Paul Fox** is the English actor whose screen credits include the 1998 *Elizabeth* and whose television credits include *The Royal* and the role of Mark Redman in *Coronation Street*.

Back on American shores Jorja-an-Fox, better known as **Jorja Fox**, born in 1968 in New York City, is the actress whose television credits include *ER* and *The West Wing*, while **Matthew Fox** is the actor whose credits include the 2008 *Vantage Point* and, from 2013, *World War Z*.

Born in 1966 in Abington, Pennsylvania he shared the 2006 Screen Actors Guild Award for Outstanding Performance by an Ensemble in a Drama Series for his role in *Lost*.

Born in 1986 in Oak Ridge, Tennessee, **Megan Fox** is the actress and model whose credits include the 2004 *Confessions of a Teenage Drama Queen*, the 2007 *Transformers* and, from 2009, the lead role in *Jennifer's Body*.

Behind the camera lens, Wilhelm Fuchs was the early twentieth century film executive better known as **William Fox**.

Born in 1879, he was aged just less than one year when his family immigrated to the United States from Germany and settled in New York City.

After having worked in various jobs that included newsboy and in the fur and garment industry, his love of theatre and film led him through dint of hard effort to set up his own theatre chain that screened films for which he had bought distribution rights.

His enterprise flourished and in 1915 he founded the Fox Film Corporation and, in 1928, Fox Movietone News.

Disaster struck a year later, however, through the Wall Street Crash and what became a protracted legal battle over a government anti-trust, or monopolies, action.

Declared bankrupt in 1936 and sentenced to six months' imprisonment for perjury, he retired and died a broken man in 1952 – with no-one from the film industry even attending his funeral.

In 1935 meanwhile, Fox Film Corporation had been merged with Twentieth Century Pictures to form 20th Century-Fox.

This, in turn, was merged in 1985 into media tycoon Rupert Murdoch's News Corporation – with the Fox name retained for enterprises such as Fox News.

Born in 1925, Paul Fox, more properly known as **Sir Paul Fox**, is the British television executive who served as Controller of the BBC from 1967 to 1973.

Responsible for the commissioning of popular programmes that include *Dad's Army*, *Parkinson* and *The Two Ronnies*, he worked from 1986 to 1988 as chairman of ITN.

Managing director of BBC Network Television from 1988 to 1991, he was awarded a CBE in 1985 and a knighthood in 1991 for his services to broadcasting.

Winner of three Academy awards for Best Art Director – for the 1953 *The Robe*, the 1956 *The King and I* and, from 1963, *Cleopatra*, **Paul Fox** was the American set decorator born in 1898 and who died in 1972.

Bearers of the Fox name have also excelled in the highly competitive world of sport.

Born in 1933 in Sharlston, West Riding of Yorkshire, **Peter Fox** is the former rugby league footballer who, in addition to playing during the 1950s and 1960s for teams that include Sharlston Rovers, Kingston Rovers and Wakefield Trinity, also enjoyed a successful career as a coach.

He is the brother of the rugby league players **Paul Fox**, born in 1935 and who died in 2008 and **Neil Fox**, born in 1939.

On the football pitch **Danny Fox**, born in 1986 in Winsford, Cheshire is the left-back who played for England at under-21 international level and, through his grandfather, also qualified to represent Scotland; he has played for teams that include Aston Villa and Scottish Premier League team Celtic.

An inaugural member of the Norwich City F.C. Hall of Fame, **Ruel Fox** is the former footballer who played for teams that include Norwich City, Newcastle United and Tottenham Hotspur between 1986 and 2002.

Born in Ipswich in 1968, he has also been chairman of the Ipswich-based club Whitton United.

From sport to music, **Paul Fox**, born in 1951 and who died in 2007, was the English singer and guitarist best known as a member of the punk band The Ruts.

Born Richard Mullet in 1976 in Cardiff, **James Fox** is the Welsh singer, pianist and guitarist who represented the United Kingdom at the 2004 Eurovision Song Contest with *Hold Onto Our Love*, and was placed 16th in the contest.

The song enjoyed success in the UK charts, as did his 2008 *Bluebirds Flying High* – adopted as the Cardiff City Football Club FA Cup Final Song.

Born in 1966 in Islington, London, Samantha Karen Fox is better known as **Sam Fox** – the singer, songwriter, actress and former glamour model who had chart success in 1986 with *Touch Me (I Want Your Body)*.

With her first Page 3 topless photograph appearing in the *Sun* in 1983, she won the newspaper's "Page 3 Girl of the Year Award" for three consecutive years.

Also in the world of entertainment, **Harry Fox** has a rather unusual claim to fame.

Born Arthur Carringford in 1882 in California, the vaudeville dancer, actor and comedian is credited by some as having given his name to the popular dance The Fox Trot.

It was while appearing in vaudeville in about 1914 that his dance steps are said to have been noted and recorded by the dance instructor F.L. Clendenen.

The jury still remains out on the veracity of the tale. Fox, who appeared in a number of silent films including the *Beatrice Fairfax* series with the actress Grace Darling, died in 1959.